IRISH REPUBLICAN MURALS

PHOTOGRAPHS BY KEVIN TRAYNOR

The following photographs are property of Aisling photography and Kevin Traynor

Aisling Photography Publishing

Belfast

www.aislingphotography.co.uk

Kevin Traynor asserts the moral right to be identified as the author of this work.
Nationalist Murals of Northern Ireland 2008

ISBN 978-0-9556950-0-1

All rights reserved. No part of this publication may be reproduced, stored in a retrieval system, or transmitted, in any form or by any means, electronic, mechanical, photocopying, recording or otherwise, without the prior permission of the publishers.

CIVIL RIGHTS

ONE MAN ONE VOTE

JOBS NOT CREED

ANTI SECTARIAN

An Gorta Mór

'They buried us without shroud or coffin'
— S. Heaney

EVICTION　　　　　　　　　　　EMIGRATION

COLLUSION IS NOT AN ILLUSION

10 people from Ardoyne were murdered by weapons imported by the British Government from South Africa by their agent Brian Nelson in January 1988 until 1994

The consignment of weapons smuggled in by Nelson........
200 AK47 rifles
90 Browning 9mm pistols
500 Grenades
30,000 Rounds of ammunition
1 Dozen RPG7 rocket launchers and warheads

IT IS STATE MURDER

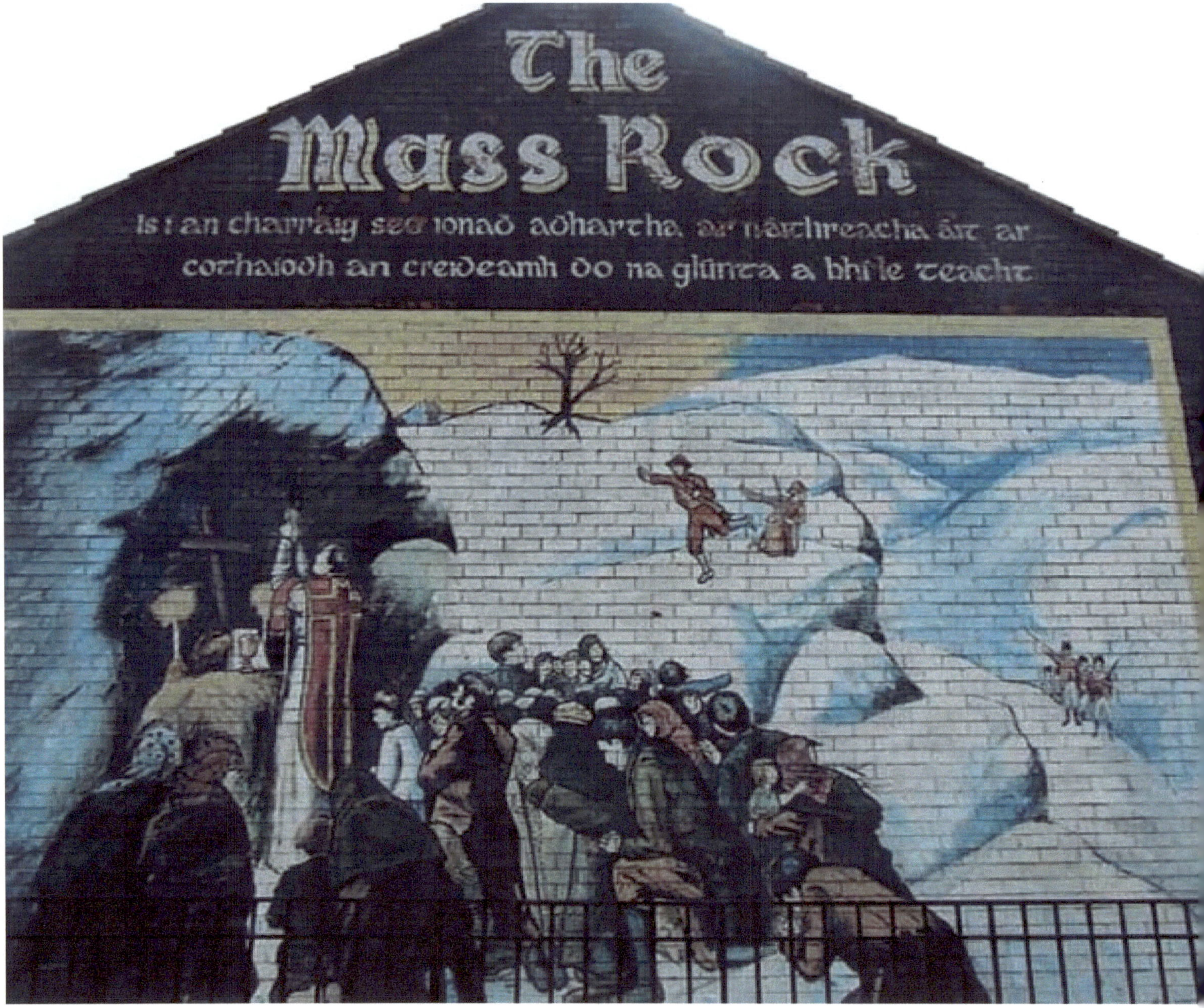
The Mass Rock
Is í an charraig seo ionad adhartha, ar náithreacha áit ar
cothaíodh an creideamh do na glúnta a bhí le teacht

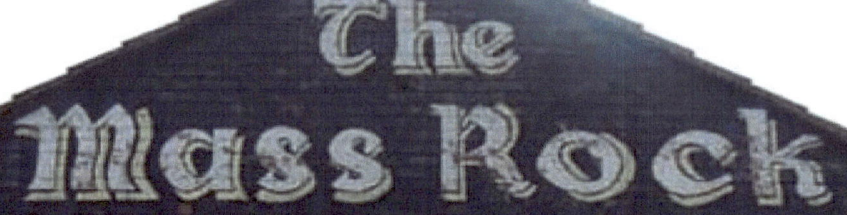

FREE CATALONIA

SINCE 1714 THE CATALAN NATION IS MILITARY OCCUPIED FOR THE SPANISH AND FRENCH STATES.

CATALONIA HAS THEIR OWN CULTURE, LANGUAGE AND HISTORY. OUR COUNTRY HAVE MORE THAN 1000 YEARS OF HISTORY AS A NATION. THE CATALAN FLAG IS THE FIRST EUROPEAN FLAG.

OUR FIGHT FLAG IS THE "ESTELADA". THE WHITE STAR MEANS THE FREEDOM, AND THE BLUE TRIANGLE STANDS FOR THE SKY OF HUMANITY.

FREE CATALONIA!
UNITED IRELAND!

EL NOSTRE DIA ARRIBARÀ!

11/8/97

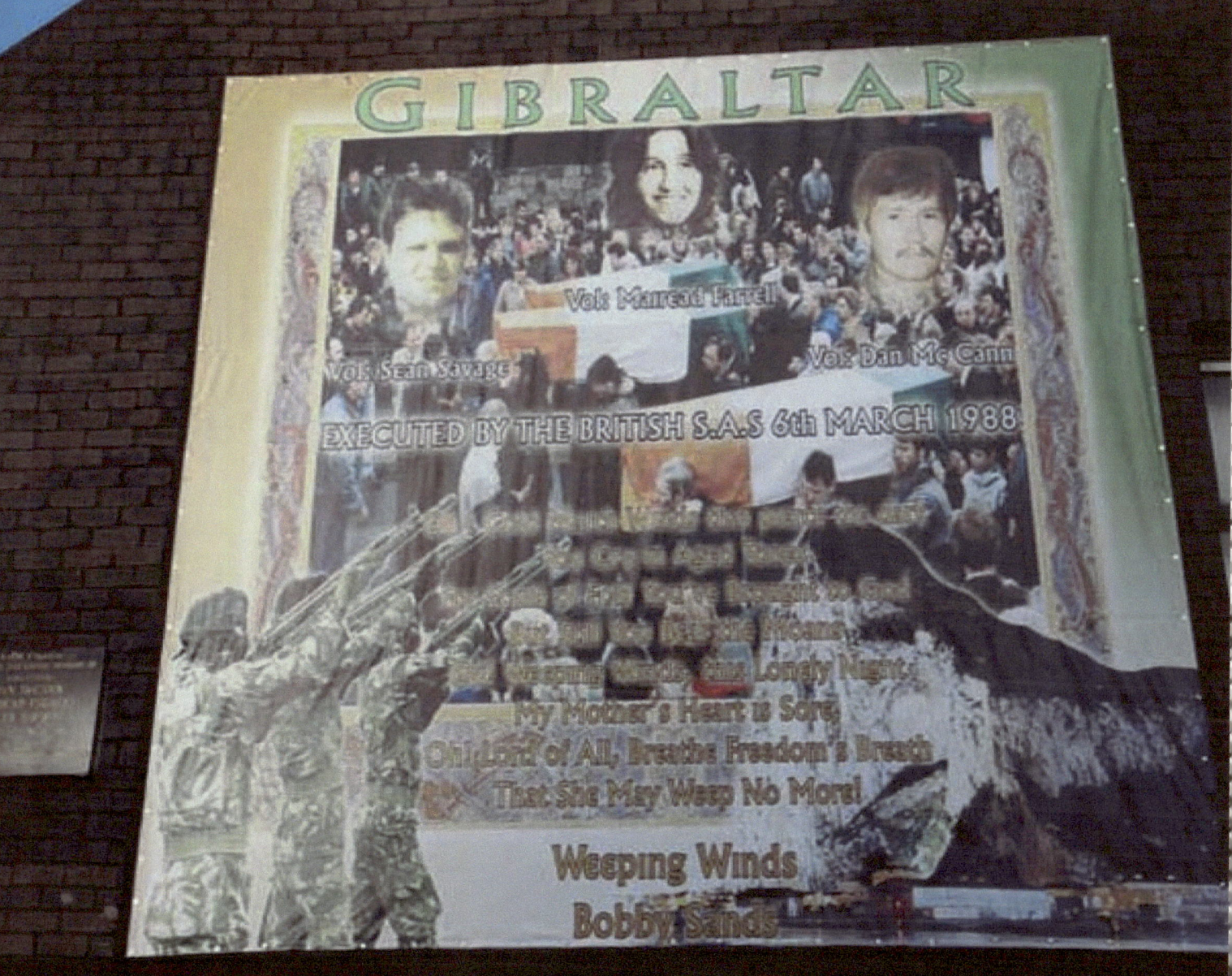

- This book has been produced by Kevin Traynor of Aisling Photography. For more information about Aisling Photography, why not contact us at www.aislingphotography.co.uk where more great Belfast images are available to look at and buy. Hope you enjoyed the book. Thanks.

This book features images from the following locations - Falls Road, Ardoyne, Ballymurphy, Derry, New Lodge, South Armagh, Crossmaglen, Springfield Road, Andersontown, New Barnsley, Lenadoon, Whiterock, Short Strand, Turf Lodge, Poleglass, Twinbrook, Ormeau Road and Beechmount.

www.ingramcontent.com/pod-product-compliance
Lightning Source LLC
Chambersburg PA
CBHW042018150426
43197CB00002B/62